DESTINATION
EARTH

TOM JACKSON

PowerKiDS
press

New York

Published in 2010 by The Rosen Publishing Group
29 East 21st Street, New York, NY 10010

U.S. Editor: Kara Murray

Library of Congress Cataloging-in-Publication Data

Jackson, Tom.
  Destination Earth / Tom Jackson. — 1st ed.
    p. cm. — (Destination solar system)
  Includes index.
  ISBN 978-1-4358-3450-7 (lib. bdg.) — ISBN 978-1-4358-3471-2 (pbk.) —
ISBN 978-1-4358-3472-9 (6-pack)
  1. Earth—Juvenile literature. I. Title.
  QB631.4.J33 2010
  525—dc22

                                        2009005015

Manufactured in China

CONTENTS

>>>>>>> >>>>>>>

WHERE IS EARTH?

Earth is the largest planet in the inner **solar system**. Like the other three inner planets, it is made of rock—but unlike the others, it is also covered in water.

Earth is the third planet from the Sun. Like all the other planets, it moves around the Sun along an oval path, called an **orbit**. On average Earth is about 93 million miles (150 million km) from the Sun, but that distance varies slightly throughout the year.

Earth's year lasts just over 365 days. That is the time it takes for the planet to complete one orbit around the Sun. Earth's day is 24 hours long. That is the time it takes for the planet to **rotate** once on its **axis**. This rotation from west to east is what makes

● ▪ ▪ ▪ ▪ **This artwork shows the planets of the inner solar system: Mercury, Venus, Earth, and Mars. You can also see the asteroid belt and the Moon as it orbits Earth.**

DISTANCE FROM THE SUN

Earth is the third of the four rocky planets, which are closest to the Sun. The next four planets are made from clouds of gas or balls of ice. The dwarf planet Pluto is made from ice.

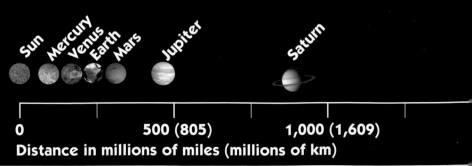

Sun Mercury Venus Earth Mars Jupiter Saturn

| 0 | 500 (805) | 1,000 (1,609) |

Distance in millions of miles (millions of km)

Your mission to explore Earth will begin in space. You travel there aboard a space shuttle, which gives you your first view of planet Earth.

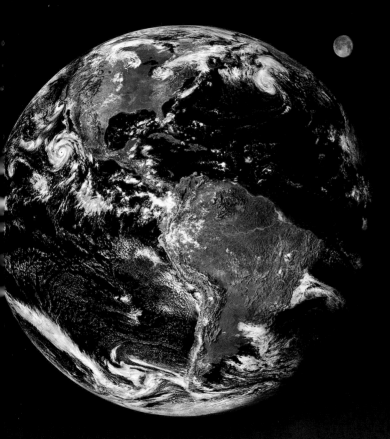

the Sun appear to rise each morning, move west across the sky, and then set in the evening. The Sun is not moving at all. It is the surface of the Earth that is on the move. It points toward the Sun by day and faces away at night.

At 7,926 miles (12,756 km) across, Earth is the fifth-largest planet and it is the largest one that is made of rock. There is another thing that makes Earth very special indeed. It is the only place in the universe where we know that life exists!

Imagine you are about to start a **mission** to explore planet Earth. On the journey you will visit space, the ocean floor, deserts, and ice caps.

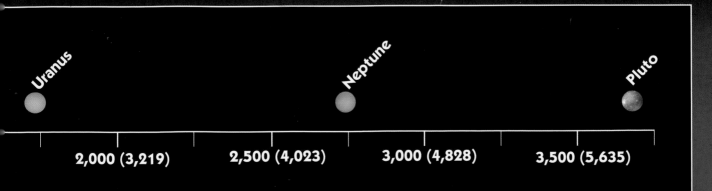

Uranus

Neptune

Pluto

2,000 (3,219)   2,500 (4,023)   3,000 (4,828)   3,500 (5,635)

A WORLD TOUR

You have traveled to a space station in orbit above Earth so you can get a view of the planet from space.

LOOKING DOWN

The space shuttle blasted you away from Earth's **gravity** and into space in less than ten minutes. You are now weightless, floating by a window in the space station. The planet below looks mainly blue, streaked with white clouds that block out the surface in places. You are flying over the Pacific Ocean and have trouble seeing any land at all. Then you reach the west coast of North America, and the colors change to brown, green, and gray.

The space station is positioned about 190 miles (300 km) above the surface. It orbits the planet every 90 minutes.

WATER PLANET

Nevertheless, within 15 minutes you are flying over water again. This time you fly over the Atlantic Ocean as you head for Africa. Your instruments tell you that 70 percent of Earth is covered in water, most of which is more than 1 mile (2 km) deep.

LIQUID SURFACE

Water exists on other planets and moons, but it is always frozen as ice on the surface or mixed into the **atmosphere** as water vapor. Earth is the only place that has a surface of liquid water, it only becomes frozen at the **poles**. What is it about Earth that makes it a water planet?

JUST RIGHT

After a few orbits your sensors tell you that average surface **temperature** is about 59 °F (15 °C), well above the freezing point of water. Earth is just the right distance from the Sun for liquid water to exist there. Any nearer and its surface would be too hot, like Venus's. Any farther away and Earth would be a cold, dry desert, like Mars.

The Moon is a quarter as wide as Earth, making it the largest moon in comparison to its parent planet. Only the dwarf planet Pluto has a larger moon than Earth.

This spiral of clouds is a hurricane, the most powerful type of storm in Earth's atmosphere. The 500-mile (805 km) wide storm can produce winds of 155 miles per hour (250 km/h).

EARTH'S ATMOSPHERE

It is now time to head back to the surface. A spacecraft will take you through the upper atmosphere. Then you plan to jump out!

THIN AIR

Earth's atmosphere stretches far into space. In fact, the space station you are visiting is orbiting in an area called the ionosphere. This region of very thin air stretches up 430 miles (690 km). From there, the atmosphere slowly disappears completely.

Earth's clouds are made from water droplets that cling to the surface of tiny specks of dust.

AIR BLANKET

Earth's atmosphere acts like a blanket. It stops heat from leaking out into space but also shields the surface from hot sunlight. Without air, Earth would have freezing nights followed by sizzling days. However, Earth has not always been like it is today. About 700 million years ago, the Sun cooled, turning Earth completely icy and snowy (below).

As well as being protected by the atmosphere, Earth is shielded from the Sun's radiation by its magnetic field. This invisible force field creates a shell around the planet (left). The solar wind is forced to travel around Earth instead of blasting the planet with high-energy rays. However, some of the solar wind does hit the air above the poles and creates colorful auroras.

HEADING DOWN

You fly down into the atmosphere aboard a small rocket-powered plane. At 52 miles (85 km) up, you reach the **mesosphere**. It is very cold outside, but the outside of your plane is getting very hot. The **friction** of the air rubbing past would burn up your plane if it was not fitted with a heat shield.

At 30 miles (50 km) up, the air has warmed to just below freezing. This is the top of the **stratosphere**. Soon you pass through the thin **ozone** layer, which shields Earth from harmful **ultraviolet light**.

TIME TO JUMP

You will make the rest of the journey by parachute. After leaping from the cockpit, you free-fall for a few minutes and are soon moving faster than a jumbo jet!

As you fall, a handheld detector takes measurements of the atmosphere. The air is gradually getting thicker. It is 78 percent nitrogen and 21 percent oxygen. The rest is made up of argon and water vapor. As you get closer to the ground, you also detect tiny amounts of carbon dioxide and methane.

As you drop through the stratosphere, the air is getting colder. It reaches -110 °F (-80 °C) as you pass into the lowest part of the atmosphere, the troposphere. This region is 11 miles (18 km) thick and has 80 percent of Earth's air in it. The troposphere is also where all of Earth's rain, wind, and other weather happens.

You fall to a height of 3 miles (5 km) before it is safe to open the chute. The air warms up again as you float down toward your landing site.

Once safely on the ground, you look at the measurements that you collected during the jump. Something does not add up. Earth is hotter than it should be. The carbon dioxide and other gases in the air allow the Sun's light through to Earth's surface. However, they stop any heat from reflecting back into space in the same way the glass of a greenhouse traps heat. Without these greenhouse gases, Earth would be 63 °F (35 °C) colder than it is now and mostly frozen.

Earth's strongest winds occur in tornadoes. These whirlwinds are only a few hundred feet (m) across but the air inside is traveling at 200 miles per hour (320 km/h).

Spring

Summer

Fall

Winter

Every year, Earth goes through four seasons. Summer has long days and short nights, so it is warm. Winter is cold because the nights are much longer than the days. In spring and fall, the days and nights are about the same lengths.

The seasons are caused by the way Earth rotates at an angle. As a result, one pole is always tilted toward the Sun, while the other points away. When the North Pole is facing the Sun, it is summer in the northern hemisphere and winter in the south. The tilt of Earth means that the Sun is shining above the surface for longer in summer than in winter.

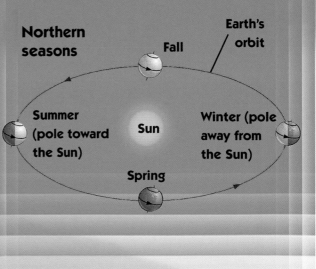

Northern seasons

Fall

Earth's orbit

Summer (pole toward the Sun)

Sun

Winter (pole away from the Sun)

Spring

IN THE OCEAN

A minisubmarine will take you on a voyage into the deep ocean.

The next part of the mission takes you into the ocean. Even today we know more about the surface of some planets than we do about what lies at the bottom of our own oceans.

HIDDEN LANDSCAPE

The parachute landing site is by the Pacific Ocean in southern California. You will now travel to Hawaii aboard a submarine and explore the ocean floor. The landscape beneath the waves is just as rocky as the land above them. As you leave the dock, a small earthquake shakes the coastline. It is time to dive!

ON THE SHELF

The average depth of Earth's oceans is about 2.5 miles (4 km), but the sea is much shallower near the coast. The seabed here is called the **continental shelf**. It is the very edge of the **continent**, a large section of Earth's surface that rises above the ocean forming dry land.

INTO THE DEEP

About 40 miles (65 km) out to sea, the seafloor suddenly drops away, forming a tall cliff called the continental slope. At the bottom is the deep seafloor.

DEEP FLOOR

At the bottom of the slope, it is pitch-black. No sunlight can reach this far down from the surface. You turn on powerful lights and head farther away from the coast. For many hours, you travel across a flat area covered in sand and mud. Your instruments tell you that the **crust** of rock under the ocean floor is much thinner than the continental crust.

This 3-D map shows the coast (pink) of Los Angeles, California, and its continental shelf (green).

Ocean waves are caused by wind blowing over water far from land. The waves break when the water becomes too shallow for them to fit.

IN HOT WATER

As you near Hawaii, the ocean floor falls away into a deep trench. While you are exploring the rim, an alarm sounds—your instruments show that you are traveling through boiling water! Outside you can see that you have passed close to a hydrothermal vent, an undersea spring heated by volcanic activity.

GIANT VOLCANO

On the far side of the trench, a steep volcano rises all the way to the surface. The only way to go is up. You have arrived at Mauna Kea, a volcano that makes up part of the island of Hawaii. You measure

Kilauea is one of the volcanoes in Hawaii. It is the largest active crater in the world.

its base as being 19,678 feet (5,998 m) under the sea. At the surface, Mauna Kea just keeps going up. It rises another 13,796 feet (4,205 m). That makes it more than 6 miles (10 km) from peak to base, which means Mauna Kea is the world's tallest—but not the highest—mountain!

UNDERWATER MOUNTAINS

It is time to leave the submarine and fly to another volcanic island—Iceland in the Atlantic Ocean. Iceland is actually part of the longest mountain range on Earth—the Mid-Atlantic Ridge. The ridge of mountains runs from near the North Pole all the way around southern Africa to India, but most of the peaks are deep under water. The Mid-Atlantic Ridge breaks the surface only at Iceland and a few other islands.

HEADING NORTH

From Iceland, you head toward the Arctic ice aboard an icebreaker. Soon you cross the **Arctic Circle**. North of this line, it is always cold because the Sun does not rise for days on end during winter. At the North Pole, it is night for six months of the year. (In summer, the day lasts this long.) Sunlight has to shine through more air to reach the poles, which also keeps the temperature low.

Once you reach the frozen sea, you smash through it as far as you can until the ice gets too thick. Arctic ice is 13 feet (4 m) thick. The ice in Antarctica forms on top of land and is 6,600 feet (2,000 m) thick in some places!

The Arctic Ocean is frozen for most of the year.

ACROSS THE LAND

With your ship stuck in the ice, you lower an all-terrain truck onto the ice and set off in search of some dry land.

HEADING UPRIVER

It is rough driving across the ice—and dangerous! If you fell through the thin ice, the cold sea would kill you in a few minutes. You are very glad when you see dry cliffs on the horizon, and soon you are driving up a river valley on top of a frozen river.

ACROSS COUNTRY

Until now the ice around you was frozen salt water, but the river has freshwater. It is filled by rainwater falling far inland. It should be good to drink. While you melt some river ice on your stove, you take a look around.

Soon the river ice will be too thin to drive on. You decide to head out of the valley. The ground is too uneven for the truck, so you radio for a helicopter to pick you up. Your map shows that you have a lot of ground to cover.

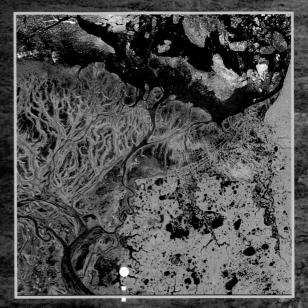

A satellite has taken this image of Alaska's Yukon Delta, where the river splits into many channels and flows into an icy sea.

Conifer trees are well suited to cold weather. Their needle-shaped leaves do not freeze easily and heavy snow tumbles off the trees' sloped shape.

In summer, the surface snow on the tundra melts. The meltwater cannot trickle into the frozen soil and instead forms muddy pools.

OVER THE TUNDRA

From the coast the land is a flat and frozen region called tundra. It is never warm enough for the soil to melt completely, so it is called **permafrost**. Only small plants, such as moss, can grow here. Trees cannot put down deep roots in the frozen ground.

AN ENDLESS FOREST

As you head south, it begins to snow, and the empty tundra is gradually filled with trees. Soon you are flying over a great forest of conifer trees. This is a boreal forest, or taiga. Although it is still cold, this region gets warm and wet enough in summer for trees to grow.

The region you are crossing in northern Asia has the largest forest on Earth. It stretches almost halfway around the planet, from Scandinavia to Siberia.

OVER THE PLAINS

Eventually, the forest changes to a vast, rolling grassland with only a few trees. Trees are rare here, not because it is cold, but because it is too dry. Such grasslands have several names, including steppe, prairie, pampas, and savanna.

MOUNTAIN RANGE

The grassland is not completely dry. There is a wide river running across it, flowing north to the ocean. You want to see where the river came from and fly south.

Your instruments tell you that the land below you is rising steadily. Then in the distance you can see Earth's largest mountain range, the Himalayas. The helicopter cannot fly over the tallest snow-capped peaks, so you are forced to change course, still wondering how such sharp peaks could form.

Rain forests are crowded with trees. They grow near the equator, where it is both warm and wet.

The Himalayas' Mount Everest is the highest peak on Earth. It is 5.5 miles (8.9 km) above sea level.

Earth's highest temperature, about 136 °F (58 °C), was recorded in a desert.

As rivers and other streams flow over the ground, the water wears away the rocks. This process, called erosion, shapes Earth's landscape. A good example is a waterfall. Here soft rock has been eroded faster than hard rock, making a cliff in the riverbed. The largest set of waterfalls is the Iguaçu Falls, in South America (below), which are 1.7 miles (2.7 km) wide.

DRY AND WET

As you search for a route through the mountains, you enter a huge basin in the mountains. It is filled with a sandy desert that is much like the surface of Mars. The mountains around this region stop rain clouds from blowing in.

South of the mountains, you enter the **tropics**. Here, the weather is warmer and very wet. Thick jungles cover the land.

WHAT'S INSIDE EARTH?

It is not possible to take a look at the inside of Earth. However, we can figure out what is down there by understanding the surface.

WATCHING WAVES

Most of what we know about the inside of our planet comes from studying earthquakes. The shock waves from quakes move around inside Earth and give us clues as to what materials are down there. Most of what we know about the structure of other planets comes from the lessons we learned while studying Earth.

For the first 1.5 billion years, Earth was dry. The Moon was also much nearer than it is now.

HOT BEGINNINGS

Earth formed about 4.5 billion years ago from the **debris** left over from the formation of the Sun. The young Earth was frequently hit by **comets** and **meteorites**. The energy from these collisions heated Earth so much that it became a **molten** ball.

Heavy metals sank to the center of the globe, while lighter **minerals** floated to the surface. As Earth cooled, the minerals formed a rocky crust. However, **radioactivity** in the metal **core** kept it hot. The outer core is still liquid, but the inner core is squeezed by Earth's weight so much that it has become solid.

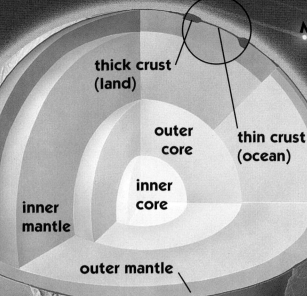

thick crust
(land)

outer
core

thin crust
(ocean)

inner
core

inner
mantle

outer mantle

MIDDLE SECTION

The region between the crust and core is called the **mantle**. This is made up of hot minerals. The inner mantle is completely melted. However, the outer mantle is a partially melted sludge of minerals, called **magma**. The crust floats on top of the magma.

Pressure from inside Earth forces magma through cracks in the crust, forming volcanoes. When the magma erupts on the surface, it is called lava.

This diagram shows the inside of Earth. The circled section shows a close-up of the crust. Earth's rocky crust is very thin. The shell of an egg is thicker by comparison.

CHANGING LANDSCAPES

The trench running through the Californian desert is the San Andreas Fault. The fault is where the North American Plate meets the Pacific Plate.

Earth's continents and oceans are on the move, changing the planet's surface features.

CONSTANT SHIFTING

Earth's landscape is changing very slowly. The land you live on now could have been a seabed in the distant past, or it might have been the inside of a mountain range that was **eroded** away over many millions of years.

Some of the changes are due to Earth's weather. The wind and water wears away at solid rock, gradually breaking it into specks of clay or sand. However, the biggest force is **continental drift**. This shapes Earth's surface by stretching, bending, and breaking the crust to form mountains, continents, and oceans.

THIN SHELL

Earth has a thin crust compared to other rocky planets. The crust below the ocean floor is just 5 miles (8 km) thick. Continental crust is thicker. Under mountains it goes down 25 miles (40 km).

Earth has about 500 active volcanoes, which let out pressure that builds up under the crust.

Today, Earth has seven continents and five oceans. However, 250 million years ago, the planet looked very different. All today's continents were joined together, forming a huge landmass called Pangea. Pangea was surrounded by a single ocean called Panthalassa. Earth's crust has shifted since then, but the shapes of today's continents still show where they were once joined to form Pangea.

BROKEN INTO PIECES

Geologists think that the crust was thicker until Earth was hit by a planet the size of Mars about four billion years ago. That collision knocked large chunks of Earth's crust into space. These chunks clumped together to become the Moon. Earth's crust re-formed, only much thinner than it was before. The new crust was also broken into sections, or **tectonic plates**. These plates drifted on the mantle beneath and pushed against each other.

mountain range

ocean ridge

ocean trench

volcano

solid crust

molten mantle

currents in the mantle

This diagram shows how plate tectonics works. New crust is added at ocean ridges. Older crust is pushed down under mountains or into ocean trenches.

SHAKE AND SPREAD

There are three types of boundaries that form between tectonic plates and you have visited examples of all three on your journey so far. The first was in California, where two plates rub sideways against each other. That was what created the tremor you felt, and larger earthquakes are caused the same way.

The second boundary was the Mid-Atlantic Ridge on Iceland. Here, magma is being forced up between the plates by currents in the mantle. The magma cools into new crust, causing the plates to grow and spread away from each other.

UP AND UNDER

The third boundary is one in which one plate is pushed under another. The lower plate melts into the mantle, while the upper one rises up to form mountains. The Himalayas are being pushed up by the Indian Plate colliding with the Eurasian Plate. Sometimes a trench forms instead of mountains. The Mariana Trench in the Pacific Ocean is the deepest place on Earth. The 35,799-foot (10,912 m) hole is formed by the Pacific Ocean plate plunging underneath the Mariana Plate.

A LIVING PLANET

As far as we know, Earth is the only place in the solar system that has living **organisms**. How did that happen?

FIRST RAINS

Life on Earth could not exist without water. Geologists think that Earth was dry at first. Once the planet was cool enough for liquid water to exist, heavy rains fell continuously for thousands of years. Gradually, the low areas of Earth's surface were filled with water, forming oceans. However, these first oceans were repeatedly boiled away as enormous meteorites smashed into them, letting out huge amounts of heat.

CHEMICAL SOUP

By about 3.9 billion years ago, big meteorites became much rarer, and Earth became a stable place. The oceans that formed at that time have stayed on the planet ever since. The seawater had chemicals in it, and life **evolved** from this "**primeval soup**."

Stromatolites, like these in Shark Bay, Australia, are the oldest living things on Earth. They have been growing for three billion years from countless layers of bacteria.

Coral reefs (below) are the only animals that can be seen from space. The largest reef, east of Australia, is 1,256 miles (2,021 km). A reef is a ridge of stone formed from the chalky skeletons of corals, which are relatives of jellyfish. Corals live in huge colonies. When they die, new animals grow on the remains.

SIMPLE AND COMPLEX

Earth's living bodies are made up of complex chemicals with nitrogen, sulfur, phosphorus, and especially carbon in them. All these things were present in the early oceans. They were heated, mixed, and electrified by lightning for millions of years until they combined into the first proteins, sugars, and other **biochemicals**, such as DNA.

TRAPPING ENERGY

Living organisms are a combination of biochemicals that are arranged in such a way that they can grow and reproduce, or make more copies of themselves. They need energy to do this and that comes from sunlight.

The first organisms appeared about 3.5 billion years ago. They were bacteria, which used **photosynthesis**. This process uses the Sun's energy to turn carbon dioxide and water into sugar food. The waste product of this process is oxygen. All the oxygen in the atmosphere today was produced by bacteria and later plants, which also survive using photosynthesis.

A rain forest is burned to make room for farmland. Within minutes, a wildlife community that took millions of years to evolve is destroyed.

MANY SPECIES

Other forms of life evolved to make use of this supply of oxygen. Animals do not collect the Sun's energy directly. Instead they eat other organisms—plants and other animals—and take sugar and other food from their bodies.

Over many millions of years, many **species** evolved to live in all parts of Earth—the deep oceans, in polar ice, and even in rocks underground. Most of the species that have lived on Earth are now **extinct** but there are at least a million types of organisms alive today!

Wildebeest survive by eating grass and using its stored energy. That energy will pass to this cheetah if it kills and eats one of the wildebeests.

ARE WE ALONE?

It is very likely that Earth is the only place in the solar system with an environment suitable for life. However, are there other planets like Earth elsewhere?

DISTANT PLANETS

Astronomers figure that half of all stars have planets. These **extrasolar** planets would have formed in the same way as those in our own solar system. We have found Earth-sized rocky planets orbiting other stars, but so far we have not found one in the so-called Goldilocks orbit—where it is "not too hot and not too cold," like the porridge in the story about the three bears.

CHANCES OF LIFE

There are 200 billion stars in our galaxy alone. So, there are 100 billion solar systems. It is almost certain that many of these systems would have living planets like Earth in them. Would these aliens have a civilization like ours?

Alien life might have evolved in a distant solar system that is very different from our own. This one is forming around a double-star system.

Some people suggest that if it were possible to travel the huge distances between stars, then aliens would have already visited Earth.

METEORITE SHIELD

Life can be destroyed by meteorites. The dinosaurs were wiped out by one 65 million years ago. However, large impacts are rare on Earth. We are shielded by Jupiter's gravity, which pulls large space rocks away from us. That has given Earth enough time for intelligent life to have evolved.

VISITING TIME

If only one in every billion solar systems have intelligent life, then there would still be 100 civilizations in our galaxy! But will we ever meet? Even in our fastest spacecraft, it would take thousands of years to reach them.

GLOSSARY

Arctic Circle (ARK-tik SUR-kul) An imaginary line that goes around the northern polar region. North of this line, the Sun will not set for days or weeks on end in summer and will not rise for an equal time in winter. The South Pole is surrounded by a similar Antarctic Circle.

atmosphere (AT-muh-sfeer) A layer of gas trapped by gravity around the surface of a planet or moon.

axis (AK-sus) An imaginary line through the middle of a planet or moon that it spins around.

biochemicals (by-oh-KEH-mih-kulz) Chemicals that occur in living organisms and are key to necessary life processes.

comets (KAH-mits) Large chunks of ice left over from when the planets formed.

continent (KON-tuh-nent) A large landmass. Earth has seven continents.

continental drift (kon-tuh-NEN-tul DRIFT) The process that moves Earth's landmasses slowly around the globe and changes their shape.

continental shelf (kon-tuh-NEN-tul SHELF) The edge of a landmass that slopes under the ocean and forms the shallow seabed along the coast.

core (KOR) The center of a planet or moon.

crust (KRUST) The solid outer surface of a planet or moon.

debris (duh-BREE) Pieces of rock, dust, ice, or other materials.

eroded (ih-ROHD-ed) To be worn away by wind or water.

evolved (ih-VOLV-ed) Changed gradually to survive in a place.

extinct (ek-STINKT) When all members of a species are no longer living.

extrasolar (ek-struh-SOH-lur) Outside the solar system.

friction (FRIK-shin) When things rub together.

geologists (jee-AH-luh-jists) Scientists who study rocks and the forces that shape Earth.

gravity (GRA-vih-tee) A force that pulls objects together. The heavier or closer an object is, the stronger its gravity, or pull.

magma (MAG-muh) A thick, syruplike mixture of melted minerals.

mantle (MAN-tul) Part of a planet located between the core and the crust.

mesosphere (MEH-zuh-sfir) The middle part of Earth's atmosphere. It is above the stratosphere and below the ionosphere. Its air is the coldest part of Earth.

meteorites (MEE-tee-uh-ryts) Space rocks that land on the surface of a planet or moon.

minerals (MIN-rulz) Types of solid chemicals found in rock.

mission (MIH-shun) An expedition to visit a certain place in space, such as a planet, moon, or asteroid.

molten (MOHL-ten) Hot and melted into a liquid.

orbit (OR-bit) A path an object takes around a larger object; or, to take such a path.

organisms (OR-guh-nih-zumz) Living things.

ozone (OH-zohn) A rare type of oxygen gas.

permafrost (PUR-muh-frost) Soil that is always frozen, even in summer.

photosynthesis (foh-toh-SIN-thuh-sus) The process used by plants and other life-forms to make sugar using the energy in sunlight.

poles (POHLZ) Points on the surface of a planet that coincide with the top and bottom end of its axis.

primeval soup (pry-MEE-vul SOOP) A chemical mixture that, with the addition of electricity, led to the creation of simple life-forms.

radioactivity (ray-dee-oh-ak-TIH-vuh-tee) The process that makes heavy, unstable matter break apart, or decay, into smaller, more stable types of matter. Radioactive decay lets out heat.

rotate (ROH-tayt) To turn around.

solar system (SOH-ler SIS-tem) A group of planets that circles a star.

species (SPEE-sheez) A type of living organism.

stratosphere (STRA-tuh-sfir) A calm area of atmosphere above the troposphere. The stratosphere is warmer than the air above and below it because it takes in dangerous rays in sunlight.

tectonic plates (tek-TO-nik PLAYTS) The sections of Earth's crust that push against each other.

temperature (TEM-pur-cher) How hot or cold something is.

tropics (TRAH-piks) A region of Earth that is on either side of the equator. The tropical climate is warm and wet all year.

ultraviolet light (ul-truh-VY-uh-let LYT) Invisible light in sunshine that tans the skin and also causes sunburn.

INDEX

WEB SITES

Due to the changing nature of Internet links, PowerKids Press has developed an online list of Web sites related to the subject of this book. This site is updated regularly. Please use this link to access the list:
www.powerkidslinks.com/dsol/earth/

ML   12/09